TOM SAWYER

Samuel Clemens

AGS

Illustrated

CLASSICS

AGS®

American Guidance Service, Inc.
Circle Pines, Minnesota 55014-1796
1-800-328-2560

AGS ILLUSTRATED CLASSICS

Collection 1

Black Beauty, The Call of the Wild, Dr. Jekyll and Mr. Hyde, Dracula, Frankenstein, Huckleberry Finn, Moby Dick, The Red Badge of Courage, The Time Machine, Tom Sawyer, Treasure Island, 20,000 Leagues Under the Sea

Collection 2

The Great Adventures of Sherlock Holmes, Gulliver's Travels, The Hunchback of Notre Dame, The Invisible Man, Journey to the Center of the Earth, Kidnapped, The Mysterious Island, The Scarlet Letter, The Story of My Life, A Tale of Two Cities, The Three Musketeers, The War of the Worlds

Collection 3

Around the World in Eighty Days, Captains Courageous, A Connecticut Yankee in King Arthur's Court, The Hound of the Baskervilles, The House of the Seven Gables, Jany Eyre, The Last of the Mohicans, The Best of O. Henry, The Best of Poe, Two Years Before the Mast, White Fang, Wuthering Heights

Collection 4

Ben Hur, A Christmas Carol, The Food of the Gods, Ivanhoe, The Man in the Iron Mask, The Prince and the Pauper, The Prisoner of Zenda, The Return of the Native, Robinson Crusoe, The Scarlet Pimpernel, The Sea Wolf, The Swiss Family Robinson

Collection 5

Billy Budd, Crime and Punishment, Don Quixote, Great Expectations, Heidi, The Iliad, Lord Jim, The Mutiny on Board H.M.S. Bounty, The Odyssey, Oliver Twist, Pride and Prejudice, The Turn of the Screw

Shakespeare Collection

As You Like It, Hamlet, Julius Caesar, King Lear, Macbeth, The Merchant of Venice, A Midsummer Night's Dream, Othello, Romeo and Juliet, The Taming of the Shrew, The Tempest, Twelfth Night

Printed in the United States of America
ISBN 0-7854-0671-9 (Previously ISBN 1-56103-441-X)
Product Number 40358
A 0 9 8 7

to the reader

Welcome to the AGS Illustrated Classics!

You are about to enter the world of great literature through pictures as well as words. Now you can actually see the great characters of literature as you read about them!

We want you to know that the costumes, hairstyles, room furnishings, and landscapes have all been carefully researched. No detail has been left out.

As you read, notice that important words are marked with an asterisk (*) and defined at the bottom of the page. Also watch for the scrolls that appear now and then. The scrolls contain important information that will add to your enjoyment of the story.

Now sit back and relax. We know that you will enjoy a great reading experience in the pages that follow.

—The Editors

ABOUT THE AUTHOR

If Huckleberry Finn is the embodiment of American boyhood, Tom Sawyer is the embodiment of any imagination or mischief that Huckleberry lacked.

Clemens, himself, grew up in Missouri and early developed a lively spirit of adventure. He transmitted this spirit to his characters in a highly readable and sensitive style.

Clemens had a gift for combining the humorous with the serious. His characters are real and believable; his settings are natural. He entertains while he instructs, a trait for which the ancients would praise him.

Other books by Samuel Clemens include: *Pudd'nhead Wilson, Life on the Mississippi, The Prince and the Pauper, A Connecticut Yankee in King Arthur's Court,* and *The Celebrated Jumping Frog of Calavares County* (his first).

Samuel Clemens
TOM SAWYER

Adapted by
IRWIN SHAPIRO

Illustrated by
E. R. CRUZ

a
VINCENT FAGO
production

Huck Finn

Becky
Thatcher

Tom Sawyer

Injun Joe

Aunt Polly

When Samuel Clemens (better known as Mark Twain) had become a famous writer, he remembered growing up in a small town on the Mississippi River. From the things that happened to him as a boy, he made up Tom Sawyer and other characters that will be remembered for a long time. . .Huck Finn, Aunt Polly, Becky Thatcher, Injun Joe, and others. Here are the adventures of Tom Sawyer. . .adventures that meant fun and joy, danger and fear, and even death to some.

Clemens began his story with Tom's Aunt Polly.

Tom! Tom! If I get hold of you, I'll. . .I never did see the best of that boy!

There was a slight noise behind her, and she turned.

Tom! Look at your hands. Look at your mouth. I've said if you didn't let that jam alone I'd skin you. Hand me the stick!

Look behind you, Aunt!

Aunt Polly turned around quickly, and, in an instant, the boy fled.

Hang the boy! He played enough tricks like that on me to be caught and punished this time!

Tom did play hookey. And, at supper with Aunt Polly and his stepbrother, Sidney, the old lady tried to trap him.

Tom, it was terribly warm in school, wasn't it? Didn't you want to go in a-swimming?

He's full of the devil, but oh-me! He's my own dead sister's boy, and I ain't got the heart to beat him. . . . He'll play hookey now, and I'll have to make him work tomorrow to punish him.

When she felt his shirt, he thought fast.

But you ain't too warm now, though.

Uh. . .some of us wet our heads under the water pump. . .mine's still damp, see?

No'm. It's still sewed! I'll show you!

Tom, you didn't have to unbutton your shirt collar, where I sewed it, did you?

Well, now, I thought you sewed his collar in white thread, but now it's black.

Why, I did sew it with white! Tom, you went swimming, then sewed your collar up yourself!

Siddy, I'll get you for that!

The next day came Aunt Polly's punishment . . .painting the back fence.

Jeepers, it'll take me all day!

Tom cheered up quite a bit when Jim, Aunt Polly's slave boy, came by.

Say, Jim, I'll get the water if you'll paint some.

Can't, Master Tom. Old missis told me to git water an' not fool around with anybody. An' she told me not to paint if you was to ask me.

In another moment, Jim was flying down the street with a sore rear end, and Tom was painting.

But when Ben Rogers came along, an idea came to Tom.

I'll give you this marble, Jim. . .and I'll show you my sore toe!

Ting-a-ling! Chow, chow! I'm a steamboat! Stop the stabboard! Stop the labboard! Stand by! Chow, chow!

Got to work, hey? I'm going swimming. . . but, of course, you'd rather work, wouldn't you?

Oh, I don't call this work! It's fine with me!

You mean you like it?

Why not? Does a boy get a chance to paint a fence every day?

Before long. . . .

Er. . .say, Tom, let me paint a little.

No, no. . .it's got to be done very careful. I reckon there ain't but one boy in a thousand that can do it right.

Let me try, won't you? Say. . . I'll give you my apple!

Well. . .I shouldn't but. . .all right.

Then, he went to lead his "army" in a make-believe battle. . . .

His soul at peace, he went on, until, passing Jeff Thatcher's house, he saw a new girl in the garden.

Wanting to get her to like him, he began to show off.

He threw her a flower before she went into the house.

Say, Hucky, when are you going to try the cat?

Tonight. I reckon the devil will come after old Hoss Williams.

You take it to the graveyard about midnight when somebody that was wicked was buried. Devils will come to take the body away. You throw the cat after him and say, "Devil follow dead man, cat follow devil, warts follow cat, I'm done with you." That'll get rid of any wart.

Lemme go with you!

Sure. . .if you ain't afeared. I'll meow under your window.

Reaching the little frame schoolhouse, Tom walked in briskly.

Thomas Sawyer! Come up here. Why are you late again, as usual?

Tom was ready to lie, when he saw his Loved One. . .and next to her the only empty place on the girls' side.

It's her!

I stopped to talk to Huckleberry Finn!

This is the most surprising confession I ever heard! After I hit you, go and sit with the girls!

Sitting next to her, Tom soon learned that her name was Becky Thatcher. She soon learned something, too.

I LOVE YOU

At noon, while the other children went home, they stayed behind, and. . . .

Say, Becky, let's get engaged to be married!

It sounds nice. . .but I never heard of it before.

Oh, it's ever so gay! Why me and Amy Lawrence. . . .

Oh, Tom! Then I ain't the first you've ever been engaged to!

But I don't care for her anymore!

You do! Go away! And never talk to me again!

Tom was very sad, nevertheless, he didn't forget his meeting with Huck Finn that night.

Meow! Meow!

That's Huck! Time to go!

Meow!

Meow!

I ain't forgot that five years ago you drove me away from your father's kitchen, then your father had me jailed for a bum. Now I've got you, and you got to settle, you know!

The doctor struck out suddenly at Injun Joe.

Here, now, don't hit my partner!

As the doctor fought with Potter, Injun Joe picked up the knife.

Then the doctor knocked Potter down with the headstone of the grave.

During the days that followed, Tom brought small things to Potter when he could get hold of them.

Before long, another, more important matter was on his mind. Becky Thatcher was ill. He took to hanging around her father's house at night.

Thank you kindly, son.

Oh, I can't stand this! I hope she gets better. . .fast.

Seeing how sad and worried he was, Aunt Polly fed him Painkiller, her favorite medicine.

Tom, of course, fed it to the cat!

Ugh! It tastes terrible! It'll kill me!

Nonsense! It will do you good!

Look at him go!

Tom sneaked off. . . heartbroken.

He soon met his good friend, Joe Harper, and found that they were two boys with the same idea.

I'll run off, that's what! Then they'll all be sorry!

Nobody cares for me here, Joe . . .so I'm running away.

So am I. Ma whipped me for drinking some cream, and I never touched it.

Let's go together. We can go to Jackson's Island . . .nobody lives there. We'll be hermits.

No, pirates. We'll ask Huck Finn to come with us.

Huck agreed. Carrying supplies they had stolen, they met on the riverbank, where there was a raft they could capture. Tom answered their whistle, and. . . .

This is the Black Avenger of the Spanish Main. Name your names.

Joe Harper, the Terror of the Sea!

Huck Finn the Red-Handed!

'Tis well. Give the password.

They quickly jumped on the raft and made their way three miles down the river to the island where no one lived.

Leaving the raft on a sandbar, they hid their supplies, then went to sleep in the open, as outlaws should.

In the morning, they breakfasted on fish caught in the river.

M-m-m. . .Best fish I ever tasted.

They went looking around and found that the raft had floated away. Later, they heard a boom from the distance.

What's that?

I wonder. . . Let's go see!

I know now! Somebody's drownded!

That's it! They shoot a cannon over the water, and that makes him come to the top.

I'd give anything to know who it is.

I know. . . it's us! They found the raft and think we drownded!

At first they felt like heroes. But, as night came on, they had second thoughts.

Ma must be feelin' bad.

And my Aunt Polly, too.

That night, when the others were asleep, Tom went off.

He sneaked a free ride across the river. . . .

. . . .and made his way to Aunt Polly's house. There she sat, with Joe Harper's mother, Sid, and Mary.

It was just so with my Joe.

Tom wasn't so bad. . .only silly and full of mischief . . .and the best-hearted boy that ever was.

Quietly, he slipped inside. . . .

. . . .and hid under the bed.

Poor boys! If the bodies are missing till Sunday, the funerals will be held that morning.

Tom had to wait until Aunt Polly was asleep. Then, before he left, he kissed the kindly old lady.

Dear Aunt Polly! She really cares for me!

After Tom returned to the island, the boys fished and swam and played games.

But later, they were very homesick.

I want to go home. It's so lonesome here.

Let's go, too, Tom!

Go on, then! I'm staying!

As Joe and Huck began to leave. . . .

Wait! Wait! I want to tell you something!

Tom told his secret plan, and the others set up a war whoop telling Tom how great it was.

That's a great plan, Tom! Why didn't you tell us before?

And so they all stayed. . .and that night were terrified by a storm.

The next day, the storm over, they cheered themselves by being Indians instead of pirates.

On Sunday, the little church in town was packed for the funeral service. Moved by the sermon, the whole church wept. . .even the preacher himself.

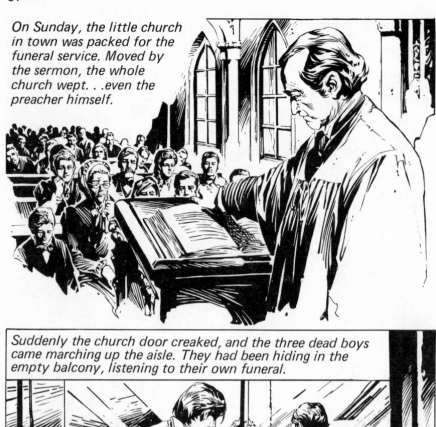

Suddenly the church door creaked, and the three dead boys came marching up the aisle. They had been hiding in the empty balcony, listening to their own funeral.

Aunt Polly, Mary, and the Harpers threw themselves upon their boys.

As a hymn filled the church, Tom confessed in his heart that this was the proudest moment of his life.

Praise God. . .and put your hearts into it!

At school, Tom and Joe were heroes. Tom pretended not to see Becky. He'd show he could live without her!

Tell us more about the island, Tom!

But after he had seen her pay attention to another boy. . . .

I acted mighty mean Becky, and I'm sorry. Please make up, won't you?

I'll thank you to keep yourself to yourself, Mr. Thomas Sawyer! I'll never speak to you again!

Soon after, Tom found her, looking in the schoolmaster's anatomy book. As she quickly put it away, a page tore.

Sure enough, Becky could not hide her guilt from the searching look of the schoolmaster.

Oh, I tore it, and I'll be whipped! It's your fault. . . sneaking up on me!

I didn't! But you'll get a beating, all right!

Who tore this book? . . .Rebecca Thatcher, look me in the face!

But before she could confess. . . .

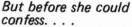

She didn't do it! I done it!

Tom's punishment was swift. . . but so was his reward.

Tom, how could you be so kind!

Vacation time came, and Becky was away with her family. Quiet days. . .until the murder trial came up in court.

Muff Potter will hang for certain.

He deserves it!

As the trial went on, Tom's conscience bothered him.

I guess Muff is a goner. But what can we do?

Not a thing. If we talk, Injun Joe will kill us, sure as shootin'. We better keep quiet, like we swore.

Tom hung around the courtroom but didn't go in. He heard troubling news.

Think the jury will find Potter guilty?

They'll have to . . .you heard Injun Joe's evidence.

Tom was out late that night. He had something very important to do. He came to bed through the window, very excited.

Huck won't like it. . .but I had to do it!

The next day, Potter's lawyer surprised everyone in court.

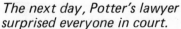

I ask Thomas Sawyer be called to the stand as a witness.

Every eye was on Tom as he took his place on the stand.

Thomas Sawyer, where were you on the 17th of June, about the hour of midnight!

In the graveyard.

Were you anywhere near Hoss Williams' grave?

Yes, sir. I was hid behind the elm trees on the edge of the grave.

Tom told the whole story of what he had seen, and as he reached the end. . . .

Look out!

. . . .then Injun Joe jumped with the knife, and. . . .

Injun Joe's gettin' away!

Although Injun Joe had escaped, Tom was a hero.

It says here that the night before you were called to the stand, you went to see Potter's lawyer.

You did right, Tom.

I told him the whole story, Aunt Polly. I couldn't let an innocent man hang.

At night, Tom had terrible dreams.

No! No! Help!

I've got you at last, Tom Sawyer!

But as the days passed, with no sign of Injun Joe, Tom stopped being afraid.

Hi, Huck! What do you say we go digging for buried treasure?

Keep still! We can watch them through the holes in the floor.

There's two of them! One's the old deaf-and-dumb Spaniard that's been in town once or twice lately. . .never saw the other man before.

While the boys watched from above, the two men spoke of dangerous jobs they meant to do.

The deaf-and-dumb Spaniard spoke. . . and the boys knew his voice.

It's Injun Joe!

What'll we do with the money? We've got six hundred and fifty in silver.

Bury it. . . right here.

Wait! I hit something. . .a rotten plank. No, it's a box! I broke a hole in it! Let's see what's in it!

Man, it's money . . .gold!

We'll do this quickly. There's a pick an' shovel in the corner. . .I saw them a minute ago

The box was soon dug up.

Partner, there's thousands of dollars!

Must've been left by Muriel's gang . . .I've heard they used to be around here.

Now you won't need to do that job.

You don't know me. It ain't robbery altogether . . .it's revenge! I'll need your help. . .then off to Texas!

What'll we do with this? Bury it again?

Yes, but not here. We'll take it to my den. . . Number Two. . . under the cross.

I nearly forgot. That pick and shovel had fresh earth on them. Who could have brought them here? Reckon they could be upstairs?

Tom and Huck had been so happy. Here at last was real treasure! But they were terrified when they heard Injun Joe coming up the stairs.

Then the rotted wood gave way. . . .

Curse the darned luck!

If there's anybody up there. . . who cares? It'll be dark in fifteen minutes. . .let 'em follow us if they want to.

I guess you're right.

Feeling safe, Tom and Huck watched Injun Joe and his friend move toward the river with the box of gold.

Whew! Wonder what he meant. . . den Number Two. . . under the cross?

They did not follow. They were happy to have reached ground without broken necks. They walked toward the town.

We'll keep a lookout for Injun Joe if he comes to town. Then we'll follow him to where they've buried the box.

He said something about revenge. What if he means us, Huck?

Oh, don't! Let's not even think about it!

Before long, though, Injun Joe and the treasure lost their importance. Becky had returned, and. . . .

I'm so glad to be back, Tom! Now, don't forget my picnic tomorrow! Papa's rented the old ferryboat!

I wouldn't miss it for anything!

Next day, as the children gathered for the picnic. . . .

You'll not get back till late. Perhaps you'd better stay all night with some of the girls who live near the ferry landing.

I'll stay with Suzy Harper, mamma.

Say. . .'stead of going to the Harper's, let's stop at the Widow Douglas's. She'll have ice cream!

The group went toward the ferryboat.

Three miles below town, they all went ashore. After the games and the feast. . . .

I shouldn't, but. . .it will be fun!

Who's ready for the cave?

Carrying candles, they all entered the cave. Soon they were having fun playing hide-and-seek in the winding halls of the cave.

By the time they came wandering out of the cave, they were amazed to find that it was night.

That same night, Huck was keeping a lookout for Injun Joe and his friend. Shortly after midnight. . . .

That's them! I'll follow them!

They went up the hill, past Welshman Jones's house, to the Widow Douglas's.

Her husband was justice of the peace. . .had me whipped! He's dead, but I'll take my revenge on her! I'll cut her nose. . .slit her ears!

Huck sped to Welshman Jones.

Somethin' terrible is going to happen to Widow Douglas! You've got to help!

Three minutes later, the old man and his sons, well-armed, were up the hill. There was an explosion of guns and a cry. Huck ran away.

Next morning, Huck again went to the Jones house.

I was awful scared when the pistols went off. I've come now because I wanted to know about it. Are them devils dead?

No, they got away. The sherif and a group of men are going to search the woods for them.

Please don't tell it was me that told on 'em! Please!

All right if you say it, Huck, but you ought to have the reward for what you did.

The same morning, at church, Aunt Polly spoke to Mrs. Harper and Mrs. Thatcher.

Did Tom stay at your house last night, Mrs. Harper?

No, he didn't.

Neither did Becky. What could have happened to them?

Tom and Becky were definitely missing. And when the children were questioned. . . .

Nobody saw them on the ferryboat going home.

Maybe they're still in the cave.

In half an hour, two hundred men were going toward the cave. For three days the search went on.

All we could find was this bit of ribbon.

It's my Becky's! She was wearing it when I saw her last! Oh. . . .

On the day of the picnic, in the cave, Tom and Becky had wandered away from the other children.

They saw many wonders.

Look!

Ugh! Bats!

Let's go down here! I've never seen this part of the cave before!

Time passed quickly, and. . . .

I wonder how long we've been down here, Tom. We better start back.

Yes, I reckon we better.

But after a while. . . .

Becky, I . . .I can't find the way. It's all mixed up.

Tom, we're lost! We'll never get out of this awful place! Why did we ever leave the others?

For hours they wandered, until they came to a place with a spring.

Becky, can you bear it if I tell you something? We must stay here where there's water to drink. This little piece of candle is our last!

Tom! Do you think they'll miss us and hunt for us?

Certainly they will! I bet they're hunting for us now. I hope they are.

They watched their bit of candle burn away, saw the tiny flame on the last inch of wick. . .and then the horror of complete darkness took over.

They slept, woke, slept again, and became hungry. The hours passed. At last Tom decided to look down some side passages. To find his way back, he unwound a kite line he found in his pocket.

He got down on his knees, feeling the way. . .then saw a human hand, holding a candle, appear from behind a rock!

Tom shouted when he saw the hand belonged to Injun Joe!

Injun Joe ran away and disappeared. Tom, scared, returned to Becky.

What did you see, Tom?

N-nothing. I just shouted for luck. Let's go back.

On Tuesday, Becky was weak with hunger. Tom went looking around.

It's our last chance.

In the third passage he tried, as he was about to give up. . . .

Looks like daylight!

Rushing toward the light, he pushed through a small hole. There was the Mississippi River rolling by!

We're saved! Now to get Becky.

After they made their way out, some men came along in a small rowboat and took them home.

A few weeks later, Tom stopped at Becky's house. Her father, Judge Thatcher, spoke to him.

Tom, nobody will get lost in that cave anymore. I had the big door covered with iron, and triple-locked.

Oh, Judge, Injun Joe's in the cave!

The news quickly spread, and before long a crowd was at the cave. When they unlocked the door, they found Injun Joe . . .he had starved to death.

The morning after Injun Joe's funeral, Tom and Huck had a private talk.

Huck, that money Injun Joe found in the haunted house. . . it's in the cave! Will you help me get it?

You bet I will! But how will we get in?

Through that hole Becky and me came out of. I'll take you right to it in a rowboat. We'll need some kite strings, so's we can find our way back. And candles, and bags for the money, and some bread and meat.

Let's start right off, Tom!

And so that afternoon. . . .

Here. . .the best hole in this country. . . just what we need when we start our robber gang.

Who'll we rob, Tom?

Oh, most anybody. Hide them in the cave till they raise enough money for us to let them free.

Why, it's real bully, Tom. I believe it's better than to be a pirate.

Tom led the way to the place where Injun Joe had appeared.

See the cross made with candle smoke? And remember what Injun Joe said, "Under the cross." The money's got to be here!

Let's git out of here! Injun Joe's ghost is around about there, certain!

Pooh! Ghosts don't hang around where there's a cross!

Feeling safer, they searched the halls leading from the rock. They found nothing. Then. . . .

Look! Footprints and candle grease on the clay at this side! Bet the money is under the rock! I'm going to dig in the clay!

Hey, Huck! Hear that? I've hit wood!

Tom dug about four inches, and. . . .

There's an opening underneath!

We'll lift up these boards, and. . . .

They had uncovered a natural crack in the rock. They crawled in, followed its winding course, and. . . .

My goodness, Huck, looky here!

It's Injun Joe's den, all right!

It's the treasure box!

And some pistols, and some other stuff! We can use the pistols for our robber gang!

Got it at last! My, but we're rich, Tom!

I always knew we'd get it!

Good thing we brought these sacks . . . the box is too heavy. Let's hurry and take the money to the boat.

At sunset they reached shore and put the sacks in a wagon.

Put these old rags over 'em. We'll hide the money in the Widow's wood-shed. In the morning we'll hunt up a place in the woods where it will be safe.

But when they stopped to rest near Welshman Jones's house. . . .

Come with me, boys, you're keeping everybody waiting. Hurry! What've you got there bricks or old metal?

Old metal.

Where are you taking us? And why?

To the Widow Douglas. You'll see why when we get there.

At the Widow's, everybody of any importance in town was there.

Tom wasn't at home, but I found him and Huck right at my door.

Come with me, boys.

The two boys were rushed upstairs, where they changed into new clothes the Widow had bought them. Then everyone sat down to supper, with the children at little side tables.

The Widow had learned of Huck's part in saving her from Injun Joe, and now she had something to say.

I'm going to give Huckleberry a home with me, and get him educated. And some day I'll start him in a small business.

Huck don't need it. . . he's rich! Oh you needn't smile. . .just wait a minute!

Tom rushed out, returned with the sacks, and told how he and Huck had found the treasure.

See? What did I tell you? Half is Huck's and half is mine!

And when the money was counted. . . .

It amounts to a little over $12,000. Tom's right. . .he and Huck are rich!

The boys' good luck caused a lot of excitement. Wherever they went, they were stared at and admired.

There they go. . . the boys who found the treasure!

Huck lived with the Widow, who taught him polite ways.

Use your fork, Huck.

I can't stand livin' like this. She means well, but. . . .

After three weeks, he ran off. Tom found him in an old empty barrel behind an empty building.

Better go back, Huck. . .the Widow's awful worried.

She's good to me, Tom . . .but I can't stand them ways!

I got to wash, and comb, and wear them darn clothes. She won't let me smoke, or chew tobacco, or yell, or scratch. . .and she prays all the time! It ain't for me. . .I ain't used to it!

Darn it! Just as we was all fixed to turn robbers with a cave and all, this trouble had to come up!

Oh, being rich ain't going to keep me from turning robber!

You mean it, Tom?

Sure! But I can't let you into the gang if you ain't got a home. A robber is more high-toned than a pirate.

We'll start the gang tonight! We'll meet at midnight, and swear on a coffin to stand by each other, and sign it with blood!

That's something I like! Tom, I'll stick to the Widow till I rot. And if I get to be a great robber, and everybody talks about it, I reckon she'll be proud!

Well, I'll go back to the Widow for a month and see if I can stand it, if you'll let me in the gang.

All right, Huck! Come along, and I'll ask the Widow to let up on you a bit.

THE END

WORDS TO KNOW

conscience	headstone	outcast	revenge
dared	hermits	raft	

QUESTIONS

1. What did Tom do to keep Aunt Polly from knowing he'd gone swimming and played hookey?

2. What is Huck's cure for warts?

3. How does Tom try to get Becky to like him?

4. Why does Muff Potter believe that he murdered the young doctor?

5. Why does Tom have the boys wait until the funeral to return home from the island?

6. What happenings in the story show that Tom was not only a trouble maker, but a good citizen as well?

7. Who surprised Tom in the cave?

8. How did Injun Joe die?

9. What makes Huck decide to stay with the Widow Douglas?